RADIO WEATHER

Radio Weather

Shoshanna Wingate

SIGNAL EDITIONS IS AN IMPRINT OF VÉHICULE PRESS

Published with the generous assistance of The Canada Council for the
Arts and the Canada Book Fund of the Department of Canadian Heritage.

SIGNAL EDITIONS EDITOR: CARMINE STARNINO

Cover design: David Drummond
Photo of author: Sheilagh O'Leary
Set in Filosofia and Minion by Simon Garamond
Printed by Marquis Book Printing Inc.

Copyright © Shoshanna Wingate 2014
All rights reserved.

Dépôt légal, Library and Archives Canada and the
Bibliothèque national du Québec, third trimester 2014.

Published by Véhicule Press, Montréal, Québec, Canada
www.vehiculepress.com

Distribution in Canada by LitDistCo
www.litdistco.ca

Distributed in the U.S. by Independent Publishers Group
www.ipgbook.com

Printed in Canada on FSC certified paper.

Contents

One
Radio Weather 11
The City Dwellers 13
Spring 16
In The Harbour 18
Red Currant Jelly 19
Shipwreck 21

Two
Neighbours 25
The Cotton Mill 26
West End Kids 28
Family Album 29
The Other Mother 30
The Gift 31
In The Night 32
Night Waking 34
The Secret Garden 35

Three
Letters from Vietnam 39

Four
The Murderer 49
Rules for Caretakers 52
AIDS Ward 53
The Poet's Devil 55
Postcard of a Lynching 56
Living With The Dead 57
New Year's Day 59

Acknowledgements 61

One

Radio Weather

When there should be snow there is rain, rain, rain,
then ice, then rain. The radio host asks

call-in listeners if they think this a sign
of climate change. Old timers hit speed dial,

side-step the point, eager to talk storms,
lives marked by weather, recall jumping out

of windows when the doors were blocked with snow,
the hospitals filled up with broken backs—

What does it mean? The questions gather. Oh,

I have another story, a good one.
This storm flooded the town then froze it in

its shell; each home a snow globe of its own.
That one felled trees older than most houses;

rain pummeled us for days until the roads
gave way, just buckled, the ground beneath us

heaved and upended, water everywhere
devouring the road as if it were a sandcastle;

took bridges too, whole towns unglued, adrift,
now islands of their own. Weather serves up

memory better than any book.
Who likes to think about means and ends,

how things change so slowly until they snap?
We fear our maps outdated, pencil sketches

on onion skin. Our stories, though,
tell us who we are.

The City Dwellers

Outside the chainsaw whirred and sank its teeth
into our maple tree, dissecting limbs

from trunk, lowering the sky to view.
It spat wood chips, then turned to larger tasks,

downed this relic of an old woman's
prized garden, not entrusted to us, but

our predecessors, the cousin spinsters
who left it wild. They kept a rotting shack

full of dead cats. They didn't go outside.
We hauled out weeds by fistfuls, only to

watch them creep back over the empty patches.
Their roots, thick as wrists, with gnarled split tails,

white flesh, were as long as twinned ermines.
The buds bloomed white too, round like Queen Anne's lace.

They brushed my waist. I snapped them as I passed,
stuffed them in bags before they had the chance

to shake their seeds. Our neighbor built a fence.
I was relieved for some outline of order.

∼

What if, I thought, we scrape the yard clean, blank
and don't have the skills to grow it back—

choose plants for the wrong soil, a temperate climate,
seduced by catalogs shipped in the dead

of winter; ignore zone guides, buy bulbs matching
the glossy magazine's seaside motif.

As if all those years in apartments, growing
my plants on fire escapes, dark windowsills,

lugging beach chairs onto black tar rooftops
that overlooked more roofs, had ruined me.

I had a neighbor who kept pigeons, flew
them every night at six. He waved a pole,

red flag tied to the end, directed them
in spirals, tight, like fighter pilots, then

snapped his flag, loosening their tether; they
flew wider and wider then out of view.

I watched them, splayed flat on my back. He knew
how far to let them go before he reined

them in, his flag drawn back. He claimed his turf,
his postage stamp of nest, sky, arms thrown wide

as if seized by revolt and waiting for
someone to look his way. I hunkered down,

head tilted back. One more lap and I'll go.
He waved his flag. I heard them first, their wings

rustling like leaves. The snap. I closed my eyes.
Listened for their return, the calling home.

∼

We bought our house, not sure ourselves of how
to stay. We who knew only apartments

and temporary places. We practiced
looking at other's spaces, exhibits

of garden art, the pissing fountains, gnomes,
the Christmas lights still hung in June, and between

what we didn't want and what we could afford,
this house. Welcomed the crocus

in their purple hats peeking through the snow.

∽

We planted bulbs in spring, the seeds in June,
tried for the fifth straight year to grow a garden.

Spanworms devoured what little shoots we raised.
I planted vegetables knowing they'd die.

I'd fertilize and weed for weeks until
the worms spun little ropes and shimmied down

to feast. I fired soapy water on them,
drowned them in beer, flicked them across the yard.

I baited, trapped, and pruned until they won. They ate
everything I planted. They got the best

of me. Then they retreated. Knit themselves
a little home. Came out fluttering specters,

soared over my pockmarked garden, without
a second look for its destruction

or their battered homes. They cared nothing for what
they left behind, nor dwelled on what survived.

Spring

The ice floes jam the harbour to the skyline,
cull the light and drive the sea further away.

I crave the spring I knew, a softer edge
of dune the colour of dried bone, squat cliffs,
low roads dead-ended by a band of sea;
not this tendrilly fog that clings to your eyes and hair.

A woman told me she finds comfort there,
shrouded in its fleece, the trees and houses
just wisps in the distance. Like an old blanket,
she said, around your shoulders. Not to me.

I bet she likes bogs, too, doesn't mind a halo of midges,
must know instinctively where not to fall off edges,
has a cellar for all her preserved fruit. I'm less
adept, it seems, at harbouring skills suited to seasons.

I don't know how to tell the wind's direction
without the radio and I'm sure I couldn't find
my way if I strayed off the marked path. I need
my light unfiltered through a bank
of white, not soup thick, with teeth.

Even most birds won't return until June.
Now its just bands of gulls, like snow squalls, circling
over church roofs, circling wide and back again,
to land on the frozen lake and tuck their wings in.

I suppose they're relishing in the wind,
the empty sky. Why suddenly I have an urge to drive

all the way to Cape Spear, the furthest point east,
where the lighthouse guards the rocky cliffs—
nothing there in the fog, but I can feel its breath,
just a shift, a warm current beneath the damp air
waiting in the wings for its entrance.

In the Harbour

Do they sneak off at dusk, when they've returned
from work, unhitch their dinghies, row beyond
the cargo ships, ascend the crooked ladders
of stages, the floorboards sagging with age?

Do they throw thick ropes over mossy pilings
as one throws off his boots before the news;
pop cans of beer from coolers saved for this?

Do they rise with the moon on their backs, lay
hands on worn wood, armed with lanterns and tools;
raise one finger to gauge the wind or see

it in the currents? Does the lighthouse bother
their intent with its silence on these waters
once called the spice routes of the East.

coloured is served in glass cups on
white lace cloths. Maybe we'll spoon it

straight from the jar, in doses, small
bites all day long, then tip the glass.

Shipwreck

It is a night of no lights,
no one on the other side of the black waters.
You pace the deck, weary.
Bird calls sound like the mad screaming
—you want to cup your hands to your ears and shake them off.
They circle, squawk in amplified babble,
until you wonder what have I gotten myself into,
this blackness, adrift on ice-pitted waters

You want the old world marvels.
The berry bowls, wooden houses,
your children in cotton dresses.
Look at the dark waters, your ship,
your travels. Your eyes heavy with sea,
hills like pillows, handkerchief gulls.

Lanterns scatter to high ground like fireflies
away from your landing, then down.
Your eyes follow the lights, the stars on the land.
Oh the scent of bread,
the soft down of bed.
You'd follow them all the way to the end
and they will lead you, past the harbour, past
the sand. Your sirens wait
for sunrise when the sea spits you back out
and clean your bones on shoals.

Two

Neighbours

She sweeps a floor that's never clean
with brisk, sure strokes that lift the earth
in dusty clouds, from ground packed smooth,
then sweeps the excess out the door.
The only light streams through the walls
that never should have stood so long,
bowed logs laid fifty years ago
on rented land, paid off in crops.
I live next door, though there's no street.
My Papa says it's quaint and cheap.
No one knows people live down here.

We hear her humming from the yard
and bolt around the back
where wheat stalks graze our arms and legs.
We strip them, let the seeds rain down,
then joust with drooping cattail reeds,
and pop the heads for ammunition.
When we emerge with wildflower tufts,
a bribe for more play time, she laughs
and scolds us, pulling silken threads
of dandelions from our hair.

We're tidied up, sent out again
for water and "sweet Jesus, peace."
We walk serenely down the path,
communicate in cricket chirps,
and drape the willows around our necks
like scarves, serve moss tea to frogs
on stumps that serve as parlour sets,
and fan ourselves with ferns like queens.

The Cotton Mill

We raced our bikes around its glass-strewn lot,
along abandoned railroad tracks, down river
and back to centre, to its bricked-in windows
unblinking against the sun.

It was a melancholy monster—
no visitors or flowers for remembrance,
only a rusted sign shot through.

Our parents spoke of rattled lungs and Monday
fever, twelve-hour shifts where people couldn't breathe,
tell day from night, the cotton dust thick in their hair.
They'd hear "lint heads" as jeers; die of lung failure.

They rose together when the mill clock tolled,
its siren loud enough to wake a town.
They lived in houses we dwelled in still.

Houses that circled a blind monster,
shoulder to shoulder near the city's border,
a river, strip of shacks with sloped, tin roofs,
and gated fields grown wild with sugar cane.

We raced our bikes around its glass-strewn lot,
along abandoned railroad tracks, down river,
heads full of ghosts and braced to call them out:
crippled ghost children and widows in skirts.

We pitched rocks at the windowless windows,
defying the shadows, ridding their stories,
which lingered on like coats of paint on walls
that haven't been scraped. We had all the injuries

of youth to unleash: schoolyard fights, our father's
worthless jobs, our floodwater pants, our lack
of anything better to do, the Holy Roller Church
brought folks even poorer than us to

the mill village. We watched them from the porch,
in houses that shifted away from the sun,
grew thin, wore their housecoats all day long.

West End Kids

They make out on the jungle gym,
grind against the crayon-blue deck,

toss butts in the sandbox, climb up
the slide, pitch empties in the flower beds.

They cruise the field and can't believe
they're not followed, double back and check.

They're the caged tigers just after
the red curtain lifts. They're the jeers

and the sleek muscle, the crowd and
the newly sprung beast, the ringmaster,

the sidekick, and not one of them
knows what the wild ones will do.

Family Album

It's not the camera we jest with, but the one
who desired us proper and pretty

and never had one decent image
to display for company.

Even in matching dresses, we sullied
ourselves with defiant stances,

turned away from each other,
as the years accumulated our angry glances

and piss-poor dispositions.
Yards of film wasted,

and to what end,
she says. I tell you, always so difficult.

We divide the photos. We're there
in every sideways grin, two

years apart and growing thin.
The girlish faces toning down,

not turning away anymore
but eyes locked on the camera.

We're out of focus, too restless
for the shutter, and gaining speed.

The Other Mother

She asks if I plan to have another,
mother to mother. As soon as I forget
the last labour, I say. I'm almost there.
It's just a story I hear myself tell—

over and over. The other mother
and I confide on the daycare floor. We
wrestle toddler feet in boots, arms in jackets.
On our knees next to the cubbies she whispers,

hormone injections for a year.
I see her milk white rump mottled with holes.
Her desperation flits; nothing works.
I tackle my daughter. She slips on mitts.

She's single-focused; her daughter's three,
perfect time to undertake a pregnancy.
My daughter's two. I was induced, two days
in labour without food, the cord wound

her thimble neck, me strapped down, arms pinned straight
white curtain dissecting my midsection.
Too drugged to hear her cry. My husband called
look, look, and I did, thankful it was over.

Then tendonitis and I can't hold her
without arm braces. Weeks of acupuncture,
hair-sized needles in my arms, hands, face,
until the pain passed and my arms worked again.

I brought her into my bed. She's still there.
I plunk the hat on my daughter's head.
The other mother nods. See you Wednesday.
She chases pleads, corners, wrestles. Gives in.

The Gift

Her call insists on nothing more
than your full attention. Her mind's a door
that leads to a door, all exits

locked long ago. She wants, she wants
to restore some happiness that haunts
her empty rooms, some framed display

she can look at when she falls prey
to her mind's circuitous flaw.
She is alone. This could be you one day.

Alone in a white condo with white rugs,
a phone book full of crossed out numbers,
the sun too bright, day an endless night.

She only wants that or this,
as she teaches you how to scratch through
a conversation, remove those words

that do not serve your mission
so that every conversation, if you listen,
comes round and swings like swords.

She'll give you all you need to live
your lifelong lesson. You learn
to pay so much fucking attention

that you've entombed all your loved ones
in your head. Never to be alone that way.
She'll give you more than you deserve.

You tongue your teeth and pray, pray, pray.

In the Night

The phone chimes in the blue-black night.
It starts far away, then nears and won't give up.
My husband turns from me, pads the floor

into the hall. It's the limber assertion
of sickness again, casting its shadow like a net.
We're hauled back up into it. He whispers

in his office as I wait. It's his turn
now to accumulate
a lexicon of terms that bear the weight

of what's too large to really know or want
to know. His voice is calm, shrouded
still in sleep. He'll return to me, heavier

and without speech, alert to what is now
a motion he's swept up in.

And I'll rub his shoulder, press my lips
to his face, remind him of how love waits
for us in the cracks, when we're dirty and blind;

that it never lets up even when we're thin
as parchment and covered in sores, even if
we've resigned ourselves and opened the door
to lesser hopes, it's there, hiding behind the curtains,
hat cocked to one side, velvet gloves buttoned up,
ascot tied and tucked in. You see it

when you turn your head, caught in the corner
holding fast to shadows. It's stoic
and tricked out for the moment.

You're its target. It hones in
while your finger traces threads
you've let unwind. Let sleep piece

them back, in finer webs, in taut
silken knots. Sleep, my love, sleep.

Night Waking

Dark thoughts creep in.
Their shadows thin as doubt.
Their steps omnipotent,
littlest dents on bare spots.

The sheets moving.
A stir, a shriek, a stirring
in a strange bed; a stranger
sleeping on your pillow.

The Secret Garden

Two years ago we found a rose
patterned plate, then another,
plainer, shard. A wasteland

of domesticity in our yard.
We delighted in the find
that our house was not

the cookie cutter kind
but a living thing with ghosts
that pass through our lives.

Three

Letters from Vietnam

Dear Sirs,

I am in the Air Force, stationed
in Little Rock, Arkansas, waiting
to go to Vietnam. Like most sane
people, I have no desire to go.
I realize I should have started
my attempt to get out a long time ago.
They don't really give you much
time to think.
I hate war and everything
to do with war.
Why should myself and others
have to go to every place in the world
and fight and never know the reason why,
except that we were ordered
by someone that doesn't even know
or care whether or not we exist?
I would rather get out legally
than become a deserter.
I need your help.

NOTE: This poem is an assemblage from letters sent to my father who, from 1969 to 1972, worked as a conscientious objector counselor in New York City for the GI Counseling Project through the War Resister's League.

Dear Sirs,

I attended an Army Military Academy
prior to entering the Air Force.
God just didn't create me
to be part of the military.
The whole scene is just too far gone.
I have a clean military record however.
I have my chick and a fine family
to think about. I would like to get out
with a respectable discharge
and sail to the island of Kaui
and do some country living.
I have considered going AWOL.
I feel like a little kid
having to sneak around
with my long hair
and being my real self. I'm fed up
with their way of thinking.
I find the thought of the military
war machine distasteful
and against the basic instincts of man.

Dear Sirs,

    I've been in the Army for two and a half years
and been to that God forsaken place
called Viet Nam. Thank God
I didn't kill anyone.
My mother died.
I went AWOL for about four days.
I was told I had to return
but I flatly refused.
My family has called me a communist.
I believe I am classified
as a deserter now. I intend
on turning myself in
when I get a lawyer.
I have nowhere to go.
Do you have any suggestions
where I could go or live?
Here is my Viet Nam patch, my VFW card
and my three purple hearts.
I'm getting sick of looking at them.

Dear Sirs,

I enlisted about three months ago
after having become frustrated
with college. I couldn't justify
spending my father's money
any longer to avoid the draft.
I concluded the Navy was my only hope.
It would keep me out of Vietnam,
pay for my education, and give me
experience in photography.
I can now see that my reasoning
was completely faulty, but at the time
I was confused and desperate.
I am sure I cannot endure four years.
I've considered refusing any orders, to RUN—
I'm afraid my convictions
are not strong enough
to counteract the disastrous
effects of an undesirable discharge
on the rest of my life.

Dear Sirs,

I am currently serving
with the Air Force,
attempting to gain conscientious
objector status.
I cannot serve a government
which wages senseless wars,
oppresses minority groups,
does practically nothing
about pollution, etc., etc., etc.
I am writing to request
some help and some
reassurance there are people
who care about not only our nation
but the world community.
That way I would not feel
as though I'm beating my head
against a wall of military minds,
that think more
of death counts and ss-9's
than integrity.

Dear Sirs,

I'm stationed in Vietnam
and face another tour.
I am at the end of my rope.
I've just about gotten to the place
where I don't give a damn.
I am trying to find some reasonable
means of getting out.
The fact remains
I was made to do something
I didn't believe in.
I have almost been killed once
so maybe you will understand
I have no desire to flirt
with death again. I am only interested
in getting out of the service
in order to lead a more real
and meaningful life.

Dear Sirs,

I believe I was illegally drafted.
My first pre-induction physical
found I was not medically qualified
for military duty. I was given
An L-3 profile. Reasons:
Polio at age five. It afflicted me
with muscle atrophy of ankle, leg,
calf, and thigh muscle. My right leg
is shorter than left. Bi-lateral Hallux
Valgus, and residual deformity.
My second pre-induction physical
found me medically qualified.
I want to get a discharge.
I guess I am like most GI's.
I don't know of any rights I have
because the people that run the show
only tell you about the ones
that can be used against you.

Dear Sirs,

I am presently detained
at Fort Riley on court martial
for being AWOL.
I was gone seven months.
It's lonely and sometimes very depressing.
You can't send literature,
as far as I know, but a book?
It cannot be about sex,
pornography, communism,
the new movements
of today, left or right,
any type of subversive material, etc.
Tell yourself that you should raise
your child with peace in mind,
and to help the world
be a better place for mankind.
God bless you, your wife,
and your almost child.

Yours Truly,

NOTE: The reference to "your almost child" was sent a month before my birth in April 1971.

Four

The Murderer

Three men kneel in dark woods. The other three
later had things to say. Who talked first lived.
In time their story became storied,
and no man could claim the last word. This is mine,

I guess. You can add a father who signed up
for visits every Saturday, brought picnics
and his child, to the state prison. My father
had lofty ideals, an affinity

for the condemned. Our prisoner, Sammy, kind eyes,
a daughter younger than me. To a child
of ten, he spoke of ordinary things.
Of the robbery, only said, his wife

turned him in. Visits were denied after
a prison riot and I didn't see him
again alive. Thirty years later, I
arrive at the website of the executed.

I read the dates—Birth. Death (method, place). His crime.
The dollar amount: small. Three men found dead
in a dark wood. One man later had much to say.
And no man could claim the last word.

For twenty years, I wondered on his life.
I put him in a house with a little yard;
a vegetable patch and wife, a cat, a simple job.
This frame I crafted until it fit him well.

And there I think of him with a child's
devotion and a child's mind for fairy tales.
A child's memory can make no sense

of finding a death row photo, a face
distorted by grief, not old age. A child's
memory has no map for this, a sick
wakening to darkness that moments before

did not exist. There is no judgment in
such a revelation. No one to mentor
such information, the story unraveled
in an instant, replaced by words

of a different language. Adult words, terror
words, words that carry flashing images
of straps and chairs, switches, needles, poison
and plate glass viewing windows, and my father

dead half my life, I cannot ask. So I phone
family friends, am given a name,
a young lawyer then, who remembers us,
the prison, who fills in details so strange

I question every corner of my memory.
The prison—now maximum security,
the progressive warden intent on reform,
the death penalty struck down a handful of years.

Old Smokey awaited its duty restored.
I wonder if the damned men felt its presence
like a compass, a needle always pulling,
the pull of steel never letting their minds ease.

Sammy chose no last word. He chose the needle.
I knew his eyes the moment I saw them,
the slackness in his mouth, the uncut hair.
When was the photo taken? His last day?

His last meal: fried shrimp, french fries, hush puppies, salad, and a Coke. No final statement. He cast his eyes upward, the report said.

Rules For Caretakers

Crumpled sheets, stained gray, shaped to a virus.
His eyes flutter open, close back into fitful sleep.
Your charge is to present the world
not as it is, but in abridged version.
A favourite photo on the bedside table, the cello suites on low.
No papers with dated news.
That will only confuse
him when he blinks at days long lost.

He'll turn his head toward you, open his eyes
and you can see they're not quite focused,
but he knows you, and you say,
you've been sleeping, even though it's been
two weeks, but now he's awake and looking,
he nods, all is back to where he thinks he left it.

Only you've grown in the hours, in
between the long nights, the days he slept, noticed
how frail he is, maybe always was, but that no matter
how far away his mind drifts, it comes back
to you. It knows home if nothing else.

He calls, doesn't trust you're there,
doesn't speak what you want to hear.

AIDS Ward

    San Francisco, 1991

This is the bed, empty again,
next to the man dying. This is

the strap that ties down
the man that lies next to the empty bed.

This is the daughter untying the strap
that restrains the man that lies

in an empty room where he is dying
on a floor full of rooms, emptying.

This is daughter who speaks
to the man who can't remember her

who brings him grapes he cannot eat
and refuses the gloves from the nurse

and kicks the mask under the bed
in the empty room where the man

is dying on a floor full
of emptied rooms.

This is the girl who unties the straps
for the man who hit her with his hands

and draws the curtain across the empty bed
and hates the smell of latex, the sight of masks

on the nurses who float past, not looking
at her and the man who is dying.

These are the weeks the girl watches the walls
instead of the man, whose skin is piss-yellow and eyes

are piss-yellow, who shakes and drools and shits
himself and who doesn't know who she is.

As the nurses push past and beds fill up fast
and empty again, walled off by white curtains.

This is the ward that speaks in whispers
walled off by white curtains from public view.

This is the floor you dream in nightmares
where the cruel man dies in an empty room

and the nurses bring you blankets
on a floor full of whispers, empty and cold.

This is the father that dies in the room
in a ward of nightmares that existed in whispers.

This is the ward people whisper about.

The Poet's Devil

We all have romantic ideas of our lives, you know.
That's how we get dressed in the mornings and leave
the house. Otherwise we'd never shave or bother
with silverware. Have you forgotten the art
of seduction, miss? I'm only a figment, yet look
at how I've handled my lot.
I brought down Kings. I had mothers burned
in front of their children.
You hear what I'm saying, don't you.
Implication. Suggestion. Don't be a dolt.
Words are power. You're thinking too hard
on all this, my ducky. You're still
going to die. And since you don't believe in an
afterlife, you'd better write your goddamn heart out.

Postcard of a Lynching

A centenarian of twisted branches
its boughs held a string for a pendulum
that only swung one way. The faces
beneath posed, arms clasped around
their friends, wives, neighbours, kids,
as if fireworks were about to begin.
And the dead man hung,
his features lost in shadow
a backdrop for the photo.

Later recovered in a wooden trunk.
Wish you were here,
it might have said. Only
it was never sent
but saved as a souvenir.

Living with the Dead

My dead don't like winter.
It's too much like eternity.
They want it always to be Spring,
the windows open and the lights left on.

They remember the pinch of wind on their faces,
twisting their ankles on rocks.

The world, they say, is full of danger. Better
to live with books and music
and the phone unplugged:
They've driven away more people
than I can remember. What's more

they lie. They rewrite history, always coming out good
in the story. They want to really discuss
their lives and what they amounted to—
the mark they left, which means on me.
They want my version
succinct and with a healthy dose of redemption,
so they know whatever mistakes
they made have been mended.

The dead don't like
loose ends.

They're healthy and tan and thinner.
The sickness gone,
grey hair returned to brown, burns
and scars faded,
the yellowed skin pinkish again.
Their bodies don't show punctured veins.
And they don't need sleep.

I should know they'd never change.
But where else does wisdom come from?
Without the fallible world, I figured
they'd learn a thing or two,
maybe pass it on to make things easier
on those who suffered when they'd gone.
They don't care for easing my mind.
They want to know if I've thought of them lately
and what I remember, and how I can possibly
love another in their absence

after all we've been through.

They want my life and dreams and future dreams
to include them all. I want this, too.

I make room for them, a corner
or a shelf for each.
And I talk to them when I'm alone.
Why should I neglect them
just because they're dead?

My house is jammed full
of those who don't want the door open
who want the world brought in
with little intrusion from strangers.
Where for whom time means nothing
and living in the mind is more real
than the outside world.

I'm happy to oblige.
It's the least I can do.

New Year's Day

Others speak. They call for time
to come meet them. We do not

speak. We rest. We look
for nothing and do not stretch

to find ourselves different
in the new year. We lie together

under wool blankets, the baby kicks
my back, pads my shoulder

with her fingers, roots for what is hidden
until she cries herself awake.

I lift my shirt, eyes closed, and offer her
my breast as she squirms into me.

My leg moves sideways to find
his warm leg. We three knot ourselves

together in sleep, content in
knowing what we'll find when we awake.

Notes & Acknowledgments

Some of these poems appeared, often in different versions, in *The Fiddlehead*, *The New Quarterly*, *Arc Poetry Magazine*, and *Homing Instinct* (Frog Hollow Press, 2011). Financial support was provided by the Newfoundland and Labrador Arts Council and The City of St. John's.

Thank you to Carmine Starnino for his attentive editing and David Drummond for just the best-ever cover.

I have been fortunate in my friendships. For all the encouragement, comraderie, and drinks thank you to Patrick Warner, Rochelle Baker, Mark Callanan, Andreae Callanan, Leslie Vryenhoek, and Amanda Jernigan.

My family never flinched while I pursued poetry. One cannot ask for more. Thank you for the love, you madcap bunch.

This book is dedicated to my husband, Peter, who championed it beyond reason; and to my daughters, Ava and Zoe, I love you up to the moon and the stars.

Carmine Starnino, Editor
Michael Harris, Founding Editor

SELECTED POEMS David Solway
THE MULBERRY MEN David Solway
A SLOW LIGHT Ross Leckie
NIGHT LETTERS Bill Furey
COMPLICITY Susan Glickman
A NUN'S DIARY Ann Diamond
CAVALIER IN A ROUNDHEAD SCHOOL Errol MacDonald
VEILED COUNTRIES/LIVES Marie-Claire Blais (Translated by Michael Harris)
BLIND PAINTING Robert Melançon (Translated by Philip Stratford)
SMALL HORSES & INTIMATE BEASTS Michel Garneau
   (Translated by Robert McGee)
IN TRANSIT Michael Harris
THE FABULOUS DISGUISE OF OURSELVES Jan Conn
ASHBOURN John Reibetanz
THE POWER TO MOVE Susan Glickman
MAGELLAN'S CLOUDS Robert Allen
MODERN MARRIAGE David Solway
K. IN LOVE Don Coles
THE INVISIBLE MOON Carla Hartsfield
ALONG THE ROAD FROM EDEN George Ellenbogen
DUNINO Stephen Scobie
KINETIC MUSTACHE Arthur Clark
RUE SAINTE FAMILLE Charlotte Hussey
HENRY MOORE'S SHEEP Susan Glickman
SOUTH OF THE TUDO BEM CAFÉ Jan Conn
THE INVENTION OF HONEY Ricardo Sternberg
EVENINGS AT LOOSE ENDS Gérald Godin (Translated by Judith Cowan)
THE PROVING GROUNDS Rhea Tregebov
LITTLE BIRD Don Coles
HOMETOWN Laura Lush
FORTRESS OF CHAIRS Elisabeth Harvor
NEW & SELECTED POEMS Michael Harris
BEDROCK David Solway
TERRORIST LETTERS Ann Diamond
THE SIGNAL ANTHOLOGY Edited by Michael Harris
MURMUR OF THE STARS: SELECTED SHORTER POEMS Peter Dale Scott
WHAT DANTE DID WITH LOSS Jan Conn
MORNING WATCH John Reibetanz
JOY IS NOT MY PROFESSION Muhammad al-Maghut
   (Translated by John Asfour and Alison Burch)
WRESTLING WITH ANGELS: SELECTED POEMS Doug Beardsley
HIDE & SEEK Susan Glickman
MAPPING THE CHAOS Rhea Tregebov
FIRE NEVER SLEEPS Carla Hartsfield
THE RHINO GATE POEMS George Ellenbogen
SHADOW CABINET Richard Sanger
MAP OF DREAMS Ricardo Sternberg
THE NEW WORLD Carmine Starnino
THE LONG COLD GREEN EVENINGS OF SPRING Elisabeth Harvor
KEEP IT ALL Yves Boisvert (Translated by Judith Cowan)

THE GREEN ALEMBIC Louise Fabiani
THE ISLAND IN WINTER Terence Young
A TINKERS' PICNIC Peter Richardson
SARACEN ISLAND: THE POEMS OF ANDREAS KARAVIS David Solway
BEAUTIES ON MAD RIVER: SELECTED AND NEW POEMS Jan Conn
WIND AND ROOT Brent MacLaine
HISTORIES Andrew Steinmetz
ARABY Eric Ormsby
WORDS THAT WALK IN THE NIGHT Pierre Morency
   (Translated by Lissa Cowan and René Brisebois)
A PICNIC ON ICE: SELECTED POEMS Matthew Sweeney
HELIX: NEW AND SELECTED POEMS John Steffler
HERESIES: THE COMPLETE POEMS OF ANNE WILKINSON, 1924-1961
   Edited by Dean Irvine
CALLING HOME Richard Sanger
FIELDER'S CHOICE Elise Partridge
MERRYBEGOT Mary Dalton
MOUNTAIN TEA Peter Van Toorn
AN ABC OF BELLY WORK Peter Richardson
RUNNING IN PROSPECT CEMETERY Susan Glickman
MIRABEL Pierre Nepveu (Translated by Judith Cowan)
POSTSCRIPT Geoffrey Cook
STANDING WAVE Robert Allen
THERE, THERE Patrick Warner
HOW WE ALL SWIFTLY: THE FIRST SIX BOOKS Don Coles
THE NEW CANON: AN ANTHOLOGY OF CANADIAN POETRY
   Edited by Carmine Starnino
OUT TO DRY IN CAPE BRETON Anita Lahey
RED LEDGER Mary Dalton
REACHING FOR CLEAR David Solway
OX Christopher Patton
THE MECHANICAL BIRD Asa Boxer
SYMPATHY FOR THE COURIERS Peter Richardson
MORNING GOTHIC: NEW AND SELECTED POEMS George Ellenbogen
36 CORNELIAN AVENUE Christopher Wiseman
THE EMPIRE'S MISSING LINKS Walid Bitar
PENNY DREADFUL Shannon Stewart
THE STREAM EXPOSED WITH ALL ITS STONES D.G. Jones
PURE PRODUCT Jason Guriel
ANIMALS OF MY OWN KIND Harry Thurston
BOXING THE COMPASS Richard Greene
CIRCUS Michael Harris
THE CROW'S VOW Susan Briscoe
WHERE WE MIGHT HAVE BEEN Don Coles
MERIDIAN LINE Paul Bélanger (Translated by Judith Cowan)
SKULLDUGGERY Asa Boxer
SPINNING SIDE KICK Anita Lahey
THE ID KID Linda Besner
GIFT HORSE Mark Callanan
SUMPTUARY LAWS Nyla Matuk
THE GOLDEN BOOK OF BOVINITIES Robert Moore
MAJOR VERBS Pierre Nepveu (Translated by Donald Winkler)
ALL SOULS' Rhea Tregebov
THE SMOOTH YARROW Susan Glickman
THE GREY TOTE Deena Kara Shaffer
HOOKING Mary Dalton
DANTE'S HOUSE Richard Greene
BIRDS FLOCK FISH SCHOOL Edward Carson
THE SCARBOROUGH Michael Lista
RADIO WEATHER Shoshanna Wingate